THE BATTLE OF THERMOPYLAE

The Heroic Fall of Leonidas I
and the 300 Spartans

Written by Vincent Gentil
In collaboration with Bruno Tabuteau
Translated by Carly Probert

History 50MINUTES.com

THE BATTLE OF THERMOPYLAE

KEY INFORMATION

- **When:** August 480 B.C.
- **Where:** The coastal pass of Thermopylae, a Greek passage between northern and central Greece
- **Context:** The Second Persian War (481-479 B.C.)
- **Belligerents:** The Persian Empire against the allied Greek states led by Sparta
- **Commanders and leaders:**
  - Leonidas I, King of Sparta (c. 540-480 B.C.)
  - Xerxes I, Great King of the Persian Empire (c. 519-465 B.C.)
  - Mardonius, Persian General (died in 479 B.C.)
- **Outcome:** Persian victory
- **Victims:**
  - Greek camp: the 300 Spartans of Leonidas I were killed, and probably the 700 Thespian allies (inhabitants of the Greek city in Boeotia), as well as an unknown number of Thebans
  - Persian camp: many deaths were suffered, but the exact number is unknown

INTRODUCTION

In 480 B.C., ten years after the first Persian War, the mighty Persian Empire prepared a second attempt to invade mainland Greece, while it already dominated the Greek cities of Asia Minor (now Turkey) and part of the Greek Islands, Thrace and Macedonia, north of Aegean Sea. During the summer, although a victory seemed impossible, the Greek cities put their rivalries aside and sought, on land and sea, to bar the way to the Persian army and its huge fleet. A contingent of several thousand men, led by Leonidas I, King of Sparta, was then sent to the narrow pass of Thermopylae, which led to the heart of Greece.

The Battle of Thermopylae belongs to the category of events that fueled European imagination for centuries, and went from history to legend. Almost everyone has heard of Leonidas I and his heroic Spartans, who stood up to the Persian Empire, at the dawn of the classical Greek era. Addressing this event therefore requires one to separate the story from the legend and, in particular, question the real political and military significance of Thermopylae: did this battle really aid the victory of the Greeks over the Persians, or has its importance been amplified over the centuries?

POLITICAL AND SOCIAL CONTEXT

AT THE HEART OF THE CONFLICT: THE MEDITERRANEAN EXPANSION OF THE PERSIAN EMPIRE

The great Persian offensive against Greece in 480 B.C. came as no surprise to the Greek cities which had time to prepare. Indeed, they had long suffered from the conquering ambitions of the powerful Eastern Empire.

The Greeks under Persian domination

The conflictual relations between Greece and the Persian Empire are rather ancient. Since the mid-6th century B.C., the Greek cities of Asia Minor were subject to Persian rule, which imposed the payments of tributes, sometimes garrisons, and intervened in their internal affairs. To control the various Greek cities, the Persian leaders would sometimes install tyrants acquired to their cause there, and would support them and maintain their power.

THE REVOLT OF IONIA

While the region enjoyed economic prosperity, the increased harshness of Darius I (King of Persia, c. 522-486 B.C.) provoked, between 499 and 493 B.C., the uprising of Ionia. Despite the support of Athens and Eretria which resulted in the ransacking of the city of Sardis in 498 B.C., the heart of Persian power in the region, the Greeks were finally defeated at Lade (west of Miletus). The repression was very severe and the city of Miletus was demolished. Darius I, who seemed to want to permanently resolve the Greek question, was preparing an offensive against the Greek mainland from 492 B.C. That year, the Great King managed to regain Thrace and Macedonia in Europe, regions that were conquered from 513 B.C.

THE FIRST PERSIAN WAR

Two years later came the first Persian War. The fleet of Darius I, which had nearly 600 ships, stormed Greece, under the orders of the Mede Datis (died after 490 B.C.). The Great King could count on rallying cities, as many Greek cities considered any resistance to be useless. However, Athens, which found itself virtually alone against the invader, managed to repel the Persians: the expected landing at Marathon, in Eastern Attica, was kept in check by the hoplites, particularly because the Persian cavalry had already re-embarked upon their arrival. This defeat did not affect the projects of the Persians, who showed themselves determined to continue their quest; preparations for a new expedition began a few years later.

Scene representing a battle between a Persian warrior and a Greek hoplite painted on a Kylix, around 480 BC.

On the eve of the invasion of 480 B.C., the Greeks thus knew that Xerxes I, who succeeded his father Darius I in 486, was preparing a new attack.

THE PERSIAN EMPIRE, A SELF-ASSERTED POWER

The Persian Empire was a huge heterogeneous space, which extended from the Indus, near India, to the Mediterranean, and from the Caucasus to Arabia and Egypt. The empire thus included the countries of the Medes, located south of the Caspian Sea and the Greek historians named the offensives of Darius I and his son Xerxes in 490 and then in 480 B.C. after them. Conquered by Cyrus II (King of Persia, 556-530 B.C.) from 559 B.C., the empire was organized into satrapies (regions), each headed by a senior official, the satrap, appointed by the Great King. Therefore, there was a satrap in Sardis, on which the Greek cities of Ionia depended.

Despite various attempts at invasion, the Greek world remained a very secondary concern for them. The offensives of the early 5th century B.C. can thus be explained by the wish of Darius I to dominate the Aegean rather than Greece itself. Nothing indicates a systematic imperialist intention, nor a desire for a universal empire.

THE GREEK CITIES: A POLITICALLY DIVIDED SPACE

At the time of the Battle of Thermopylae, most of Greece was organized into cities, i.e. small independent states with permanent central institutions, and a highly fortified city, as well as developed artisanal and commercial activities.

In the early 5th century B.C., the Greek cities remained a highly divided group, where local and regional wars were practically permanent. Sparta, which had many allies gathered in the Peloponnesian League represented the main power, even though the city of Athens, which had just adopted a new democratic constitution, was on the rise.

After the Battle of Marathon (490 B.C.), the discovery of silver-lead mines in the Laurion massif, in the heart of their territory, allowed the Athenians to build a large war fleet, the future instrument of their victories over the Persians and their dominance over Greece.

Besides these cities, a more archaic form of organization still existed, which the Greeks called *ethnos* (from the Greek meaning "people" or "race"), mainly in the western highlands and in the north. In this case, there was no capital city or permanent common institutions, but a network of more and less important villages. This was particularly the case in Thessaly, Macedonia and Phocis (in northern Greece).

THE SECOND PERSIAN WAR: A LARGE-SCALE OFFENSIVE

Since his inception in 486 B.C., Xerxes continued the work of his father and decided to project a gigantic expedition against Greece, as announced by the following preparations, between 483 and 481 B.C.:

- Two pontoon bridges were built on the Hellespont (now Dardanelles), a strait which allowed for the passage from Asia to Europe;
- A channel was dug to prevent the Persian fleet from having to bypass the peninsula of Mount Athos;
- Food was channeled to Thrace and Macedonia, which had already surrendered.

Moreover, even if we do not have precise figures, the Greek

historian Herodotus (c. 484-420 B.C.) argues that the king was able to draw on a large fighting force, estimated at about 200 000 men and 1 000 boats. Tradition states that the army marched for seven days and seven nights before its leader, which, for Greek writers, is an opportunity to highlight the excess (*hubris*) of the East.

In 481 B.C., Xerxes I left the capital of Susa for Sardis, and the following spring, the immense army set out and arrived in Macedonia without having fought, while its fleet was stationed north of the Aegean Sea. Unlike the invasion of 490 B.C., the Great King directed the expedition in person, thus being at the head of several hundred thousand soldiers that were joined as they advanced by Greek contingents raised in the countries they crossed and that were immediately submitted if they had not already done so, such as Ionia, Thrace, Macedonia and Thessaly.

THE GREEK CITIES ORGANIZED RESISTANCE

Faced with this mortal danger, the Greek cities managed to put aside their antagonisms and quickly organized a joint strategy: meeting at Corinth, they united in a Pan-Hellenic league and entrusted the command of operations to the Spartan King Leonidas I. The Thessalians, immediately threatened by Xerxes I, then proposed the establishment of a line of defense between their country and Macedonia, but after the refusal of the Greek league, they eventually joined the Persian camp. The Greeks chose to await the enemy in the south:

- their fleet waited at Artemisium, in northern Evia;
- a part of the infantry was stationed in the pass of Thermopylae.

The strategy was clear: blocking the Persians in narrow places where they could not deploy all of their forces.

COMMANDERS AND LEADERS

LEONIDAS I, KING OF SPARTA

Bust portraying Leonidas I.

Leonidas became King of Sparta in 489 or 488 B.C., together with Leotychidas (died 469 B.C.). He embodied the resistance of the whole of Greece against the Persian invasion, since it was he who led the division in charge of detaining the army of Xerxes in 480 B.C. at Thermopylae. Little is known about him outside of the conditions of his accession to the monarchy and his role during the battle in which he was killed.

GOOD TO KNOW

The city of Sparta was led by two kings, appointed from two different royal families, the Eurypontides and the Agiades, supposedly descended from Hercules. Their powers were limited, but they both had very important military and religious functions. Although it was hereditary, royal power seems to have been subject to the approval of the Spartans, with the existence of the two kings limiting the risk of falling into tyranny.

The kings shared their power with other institutions, such as:

- the Gerontes, which formed a high court of justice controlling the decisions of the assembly of the people;
- the Ephors, which formed a sort of government, ensuring foreign relations and executing the decisions of the popular assembly;
- the citizen's assembly, which elected the Gerontes and the Ephors, passed laws and voted for peace and wars, but their real power seemed limited.

Belonging to the royal family of the Agiades, Leonidas succeeded his elder half-brother Cleomenes, who died without a male heir in 490 B.C., as the grandson of King Anaxandrides.

He married Gorgo, the daughter of Cleomenes. This ascension, although unexpected, complied with Spartan custom and seemed to pass without being challenged.

However, Leonidas I took power in a context where the monarchy seemed subject to closer monitoring by the civic body:

- Whereas before, the two kings could take to the field together, one of them was now required to stay in the city, where he could counter-balance the one who commanded the army. Therefore, Leonidas I was sent to Thermopylae alone, while Leotychidas remained in Sparta.
- Moreover, while Cleomenes could still take the initiative to raise an army as he saw fit, it was now customary for the people's assembly to decide on war or peace before the king's departure on the campaign.

DID YOU KNOW?

During a military campaign, the king, surrounded by a guard chosen from the elite troops, fought in the front row of the right wing. He had several rights, such as:

- the right to life and death over his men;
- the right to conclude a truce and forge alliances.

However, to make peace, he had to obtain the agreement of the city.

This trend may explain the strict obedience to the law that characterized the action of Leonidas I, and the eagerness with which he defended Thermopylae, even though the position was obviously lost.

Was it that he was afraid of retaliation in the case of failure upon his return? This question deserves to be asked, as the king was under the control of the powerful Ephors, senior judges who applied the decisions of the assembly of the people and could demand accountability from kings on their return to the country.

This did not however detract from the heroism of the Spartan leader and the value of his military action, which was celebrated in Sparta, as well as in the rest of Greece until the end of the ancient period and beyond, as further evidenced by the statue erected in the fifties on the site of the battle.

XERXES I, THE GREAT KING OF THE PERSIAN EMPIRE

The son and successor of Darius I, Xerxes I was 35 years old when he ascended to the head of the Persian Empire in 486 B.C. and immediately organized a major offensive against Greece, which ended in a major failure.

He belonged to the Persian Achaemenid dynasty, of which he was the fourth sovereign, and ruled over a vast territory that had been enlarged even further by his father. His reign was characterized by religious intransigence, especially to the Mesopotamian cults. Outside of the Empire, he continued the policy of domination over the Greek world started by his father and sought to avenge the humiliation suffered in the defeat at Marathon.

However, the 480 B.C. offensive, gigantic in terms of the means implemented, also had a strategic logic: already controlling Egypt, the Near East, Asia Minor and Thrace, the Great King sought to control the entire perimeter of the Aegean by obtaining the submission of the Greek cities of the European side. For the first time, he took charge of the expedition himself, demonstrating the importance that he attributed to it.

The failure of the invasion did not have any serious consequences for the empire and the sovereignty of Xerxes I was also not contested. However, he never managed to reach an agreement with the Greeks. Indeed, it was his successor Artaxerxes I (465-424 B.C.) who signed the Peace of Callias in 449 B.C., which officially put an end to the state of war with Greece.

More generally, it should be noted that with Xerxes, the Persian territorial expansion stopped: he was the first sovereign to not obtain a significant exterior victory.

He was assassinated in 465 B.C., victim to one of the greatest evils of the empire: court conspiracy.

MARDONIUS, PERSIAN GENERAL

Cousin of the Great King Xerxes, Mardonius played a political and military role in the offensive against Greece in the early 5th century B.C.

In 492 B.C., at the beginning of the first Persian War, he became head of the expedition that aimed to restore the Persian domination over Thrace and Macedonia, but faced violent resistance, during which he was wounded. He then returned to Persia, losing much of his fleet in a storm off Mount Athos.

Herodotus says that Mardonius exerted a strong influence on Xerxes I, who he apparently convinced to once again march against Greece to take his revenge on Athens, which had defeated the Persians at Marathon, but also because "Europe was a wondrous beautiful region, rich in all kinds of cultivated trees, and the soil excellent: no one, save the king, was worthy to own such a land" (*The Histories*, Book VII). He also drew on the experience of the 492 B.C. campaign to convince the king that the Greeks would never present a united front and that many of them would quickly rally to the Persians.

After the Persian defeat at Salamis in September 480 B.C., Mardonius favored a continuation of operations and the rapid submission of Greece by land. Remaining in the north of the country during the winter with the best troops of the empire, he led the offensive of 479 B.C., which resulted in the Persian defeat at Plataea where he died facing the troops of the Spartan Pausanias (died c. 467 B.C.), brother of Leonidas I.

ANALYSIS OF THE BATTLE

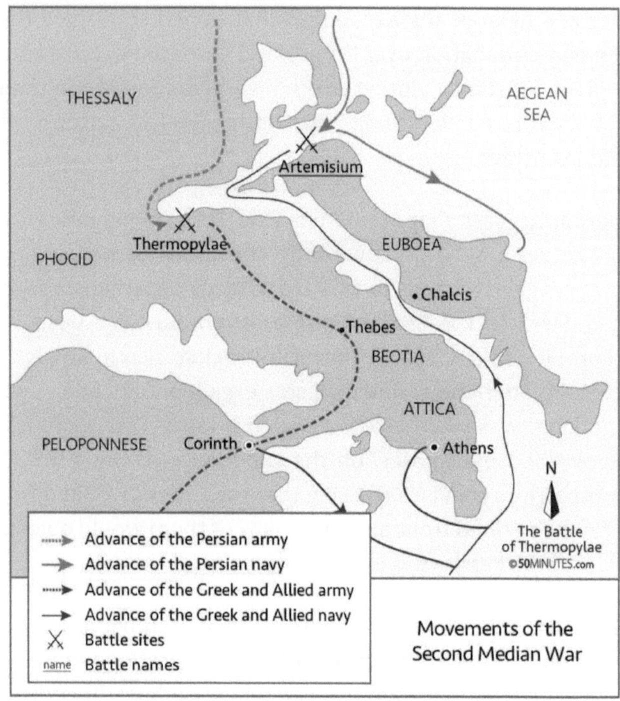

THE POSITIONING

In August 480 B.C., while at Artemisium (northern Evia), a fleet of 280 vessels, mostly Athenians, had to block the sea to the south from the Persians, a contingent of several thousand men marched north and blocked the pass of

Thermopylae, a narrow corridor of about fifteen meters wide, between the sea and the mountains, of approximately 1.5 km in length. A fortification blocked access from the northwest. The name of this narrow passage, which in Greek means "hot gates", came from the many hot springs that arose there.

The fighters were mostly Greeks of the Peloponnese and central Greece, of which the historian Herodotus gives precise numbers, although these numbers have been discussed *a posteriori* by historians: the most numerous were the cities of Tegea, Mantinea, Corinth, Thespiae, Thebes and Sparta. In total, it is now estimated that the contingent totaled about 5 000 men. Among these was the famous elite corps of the Three Hundred, chosen for their military skills and quickly sent before the other Greeks to Thermopylae to encourage them to overcome their fear. Although Herodotus does not mention it, it is likely that one thousand additional Spartans joined the expedition. All were controlled by Leonidas I, but each division obeyed directly to the military leaders of their city. However, they represented only a small part of the Greek forces, which was especially prepared to defend the Isthmus of Corinth in the south.

GOOD TO KNOW

Greek warriors were mostly citizens of at least 21 years of age, who had all undergone extensive training, which was particularly demanding in Sparta. There were several elite corps, such as the Spartan Three Hundred or the Sacred Band of Thebes, but their method of recruitment was not well known. The texts regularly mention the Spartan Three Hundred warrior elite, but it should be distinguished from the *hippeis* (horsemen), a group of 300 men who were also an elite selected by the magistrates of the city.

It seemed that the cities of the Peloponnese did not want to send more men to the north, as the situation was considered very dangerous, while the Isthmus of Corinth seemed easier to defend. Moreover, many of them used the excuse of religious festivals taking place at the time to send only a small contingent. We know that Sparta could have mobilized more than 6 000 hoplites alone, but preferred to keep them close to its territory, in accordance with tradition. Indeed, not only did the Spartans hesitate over the strategy to stand against the Persian invasion, but it was not in their ways to send large contingents away from their territory, for two reasons:

- Firstly, they sought above all to prevent an uprising of the Perioikois and the Helots, indigenous people of the Peloponnese that they had defeated;
- Secondly, they were attached to their traditional hoplite model, which opposed the remote and adventurous wars, as noted by Athenian historian Thucydides (c. 460-395 B.C.), who saw this behavior as majorly different to that of Athens.

A FIRST UNFAVORABLE PHASE FOR THE PERSIANS

Leonidas I moved part of the Spartans in front of the wall that was protecting the pass and that had been restored for the occasion. The rest of the troops were stationed under the protection of this wall.

For two days, his men demonstrated the superiority of the Greek tactics: the elite troops of Xerxes I and its general Mardonius, of which Medes and the famous Persian "Immortals" (body of 10 000 fighters that was constantly renewed) were pushed back several times by the hoplites, excelling especially in retirement maneuvers and counter-attacks. Their lances were longer than those of the Persians and their large round shields gave them a significant advantage over their Eastern enemies. The details of the losses suffered by the Greeks and the Barbarians during the first battles are unknown, but they were undoubtedly deadly for the invaders.

The combat tactic of the hoplites was to form a tight formation, the phalanx, in order to repel the enemy with spears, while protecting each other with shields, which partially overlapped each other to form a united front.

The phalanx was organized four to eight ranks deep, which prevented the front from being broken if one of the combatants were to fall. This device, which was efficient overall, had two weaknesses: its wings and its rear. This practice, which was very different from that described in the poems of Homer (epic Greek poet, 8th century B.C.) for the prior period, involved many fighters linked by a strong cohesion. Thus, it may have promoted the expansion of the group of citizens having political rights, which was necessary in Greece to take part in the war.

At the same time, the Persian fleet encountered serious problems: a portion of the ships were destroyed by a storm at Cape Sepias, while others were defeated at Cape Artemisium. This fleet that was so numerous could barely take shelter in the harbors during stormy weather; faced with the Greeks, with the rugged coastline and the Aegean islands, it had no space to mobilize all of its forces.

THE GREEK RETREAT AND THE SACRIFICE OF THE THREE HUNDRED

After two days of fierce fighting, the Greeks of Leonidas I continued to resist, but their position was threatened by Persian troops which, guided by the Greek Ephialtes (c. 495-461 B.C.), found a path in the mountains that allowed them to move beyond Thermopylae, towards the southeast. The Phocidians, who had mobilized a contingent of one thousand men to monitor the mountain, failed in this task: the Persians, commanded by Hydarnes (521-480 B.C.), marched at night and arrived at the top without being seen. The situation was even more critical for the Greeks as the long-awaited reinforcements did not arrive.

The Persians descended without even fighting the Phocidians, heading directly for the troops of Leonidas I. Before the noose tightened completely and to avoid bloodshed, the King of Sparta sent most of his warriors back to the south. As underlined by Herodotus, it is also likely that the fear of death, which was inevitable for those who remained at Thermopylae, made many of the Greeks unfit for combat. The Spartan leader therefore kept the hoplites at his side, who were determined to carry out their commitments to the end. Thus, the Three Hundred, supported by the fighters from the cities of Thespiae and Thebes, managed to hold out a few more hours, for the greater glory of Sparta, before being slaughtered right down to the last man, including Leonidas I.

This sacrifice was not done freely and did not result from a quest for personal glory. Indeed, for the Spartans, failure in combat was never exalted for itself, but must be accepted when necessary for the fulfillment of duty. Thus, the inscription at Delphi on the tomb of the Spartans who fell during the Battle of Thermopylae, according to Herodotus, was as follows: "Go tell the Spartans, stranger passing by, that here, obedient to their laws, we lie" (Book VII, 228). Sent to hold the parade for as long as possible, Leonidas I had perfectly fulfilled his mission while sparing the bulk of the troops that had been entrusted to him.

REPERCUSSIONS OF THE BATTLE

MILITARY CONSEQUENCES

Invasion of Greece

The fierce resistance of the Three Hundred delayed the Persians for a time and allowed the Greek fleet to withdraw to Attica before being enveloped by the Persians, which did not prevent the land invasion of Greece to the Isthmus of Corinth. Phocis and Boeotia were plundered, while Attica, abandoned by the Athenians, was ravaged. Even worse, the Acropolis sanctuary was burned down by the Persians. Yet, despite this disaster, the Athenians still refused the peace offerings of Xerxes and assured the Spartans that they would continue to fight for the freedom of the Greeks.

The Athenians and their allies then put everything in the hands of their fleet and, in September 480 B.C., the Greek triremes (warships with three ranks of rowers), led by Themistocles (Athenian statesman, 528-462 B.C.), fought the ships of the Persian Great King in the Bay of Salamis. This naval battle gave the advantage to the Greeks, who managed to rout the Persian fleet.

The decline of the Persian army

Xerxes I, who, until then, believed that he had gained a victory, decided to turn back and have the rest of his fleet and most of his troops return to Ionia (Asia Minor), despite its victories on land and the significance of his forces; he himself settled in Sardis (the capital of Lydia). Only the elite troops commanded by Mardonius remained in central and northern Greece. Herodotus assumed that the Persian Great King feared that the Greeks would destroy the pontoon on the Hellespont, cutting him off from his bases. However, it is more likely that Xerxes I followed this strategy according to Persian custom, as it was not for the king to direct military operations. In addition, the arrival of winter required him to suspend operations. At the end of the year 480 B.C., nothing had played out and the Greeks were expecting a new offensive the following spring.

The Greek victory at Plataea and Cape Mycale

However, the victory at Salamis prompted the Persian retreat. Moreover, the troops of Mardonius were defeated on land in 479 B.C. at Plataea (Boeotia). All the Greek forces fought, which constituted 110 000 warriors, including the Spartans that mobilized 35 000 helots (public slaves of Sparta), which was exceptional. Mardonius died during the battle.

That same year, the Persians were also defeated at Cape Mycale in Ionia, marking their final defeat by Greece and the end of the invasions. Xerxes was therefore the last Persian king to enter Europe. A century and a half later, his empire was conquered by Greece, which mobilized around Alexander the Great (356-323 B.C.).

The succession of Leonidas I and the situation in Sparta

The death of Leonidas I during the Battle of Thermopylae forced the Spartans to quickly find a successor. As the Spartan king had no adult heir, the Spartans chose to entrust the regency to his nephew, Pausanias. It was the latter who controlled the Greek army that confronted the Persians at Plataea while the second king, Leotychidas, commanded the fleet that led the hoplites to Cape Mycale.

POLITICAL CONSEQUENCES

This unexpected victory of the Greeks had serious political consequences, especially in terms of hegemony and the influence of Athens throughout the Aegean Greek world. Indeed, the city became head of the Delian League, an organization that fought against the threat of Eastern invasion. It created a fleet and an immense treasure for itself, thanks to more or less voluntary contributions of other cities involved in the league. As for the Spartans, attached to their autonomy, they preferred to focus their efforts on the Peloponnese, which they dominated, rather than on overseas territories.

A sacred battle

A sacred dimension was quickly attached to the Battle of Thermopylae, as evidenced by the verses of the Greek poet Simonides of Ceos (c. 556-467 B.C.): "Of those who perished at Thermopylae, all glorious is the fortune, fair the doom; their grave's an altar" (quoted by Diodorus Siculus, *Historical*

Library, XI, 11, 6). These words, echoing those carved on the tomb of the Spartans at the sanctuary of Delphi, would forever mark European memory.

From ancient times, this warlike episode in the history of the Greeks inspired literature, including the tragic play *The Persians*, written around 472 B.C. by Aeschylus (Greek tragic poet, 526-456 B.C.), in which he portrays the especially famous Athenian victory at Salamis, but also the "Dorian spear" i.e. the value of the Spartan hoplites. 600 years later, the biography (now lost) which Plutarch (Greek writer, 46-125 A.D.) dedicated to Leonidas I is proof of the lasting admiration felt towards the Spartan leader, right up until Roman times.

SUMMARY

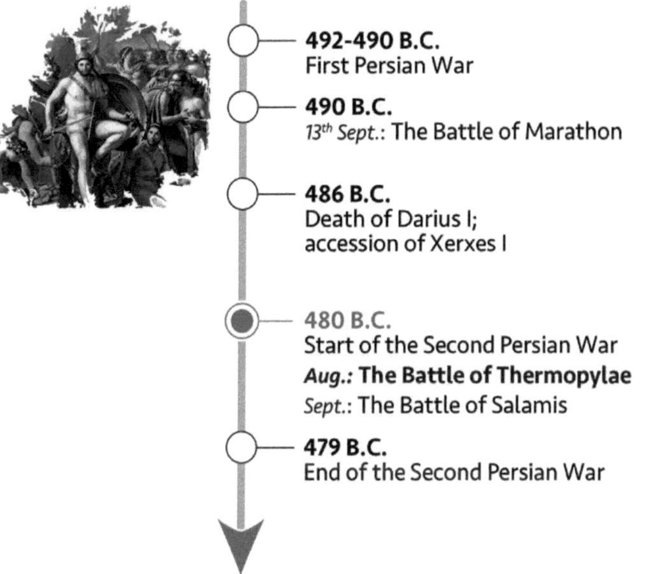

492-490 B.C.
First Persian War

490 B.C.
13th Sept.: The Battle of Marathon

486 B.C.
Death of Darius I;
accession of Xerxes I

480 B.C.
Start of the Second Persian War
***Aug.:* The Battle of Thermopylae**
Sept.: The Battle of Salamis

479 B.C.
End of the Second Persian War

- In 481 B.C., to avenge the defeat of Marathon and to control the Aegean Sea, the Persian Great King Xerxes was preparing an invasion of Greece by organizing a strong army of hundreds of thousands of combatants and more than 1 000 ships.
- In the spring of 480 B.C., the great army set out, crossing Thrace and invading northern Greece, threatening the entire peninsula.
- During the summer, the Greeks held a congress in Corinth and agreed to entrust land operations to the Spartan

King Leonidas I and maritime operations to the city of Athens.

- In August, with only 5 000 men, Leonidas I managed to slow the Persian progression towards the south at the pass of Thermopylae for two days, while the Greek fleet blocked the enemy north of the island of Evia.
- However, the Greeks lost the advantage when the Persians managed to bypass the narrow passage. Considering the desperate situation, Leonidas I sent away the bulk of his troops, but fought for several hours with his elite warriors, the Three Hundred, allowing the Greek fleet to withdraw to Attica.
- The Three Hundred all died in battle, but became legendary, further reinforcing the military prestige of Sparta.
- In September, the naval victory at Salamis saved Greece from the Persian invasion.
- The following year, in 479 B.C., new Greek victories definitively allowed Greece to be released from the grip of Xerxes.

We want to hear from you!
Leave a comment on your online library
and share your favourite books on social media!

FIND OUT MORE

BIBLIOGRAPHY

- Briant, P. (1995) Les guerres médiques. In *Le monde grec aux temps classiques. Le V*^e *siècle*, Volume I Paris: Presses Universitaires de France, pp. 27-37.
- Christien, J. and Ruzé, F. (2007) *Sparte. Géographie, mythes et histoire.* Paris: Armand Colin.
- Christien, J. and Le Tallec, Y. (2013) *Léonidas. Histoire et mémoire d'un sacrifice.* Paris: Ellipse.
- Fouchard, A. (2003) *Les systèmes politiques grecs.* Paris: Ellipses.
- Garlan, Y. (1976) *War in the Ancient World.* New York: W.W. Norton & Company.
- Lévêque, P. (1964) *L'aventure grecque.* Paris: Armand Colin.
- Lévy, E. (1995) *La Grèce au V*^e *siècle.* Paris: Seuil.
- Lévy, E. (2003) *Sparte. Histoire politique et sociale jusqu'à la conquête romaine.* Paris: Seuil.
- Malye, J. (2007) *La véritable histoire de Sparte et de la bataille des Thermopyles.* Paris: Les Belles Lettres.
- Schmidt, T (2009) Plutarque, les *Préceptes politiques* et le récit des Guerres médiques. *Cahiers des études anciennes*, Volume 46, pp. 101-128. [Online]. [Accessed 8 December 2016]. Available from: <http://etudesanciennes.revues.org/170>
- Vernant, J.-P. (1985) *Problèmes de la guerre en Grèce ancienne.* Paris: Éditions de l'EHESS.

ADDITIONAL SOURCES

- Bradford, E. (2004) *Thermopylae: The Battle for the West.* Cambridge, Massachusetts: Da Capo Press.
- Herodotus (2003) *The Histories.* Trans. De Sélincourt, A. London: Penguin, pp. 413-500.
- Matthew, C. and Trundel, M. (2013) *Beyond the Gates of Fire: New Perspectives on the Battle of Thermopylae.* Barnsley: Pen and Sword Military.
- Matthews, R. (2008) *The Battle of Thermopylae: A Campaign in Context.* Stroud, Gloucestershire: Spellmount Publishers.

ICONOGRAPHIC SOURCES

- Scene representing a battle between a Persian warrior and a Greek hoplite painted on a Kylix, around 480 BC. Royalty-free reproduction picture.
- Bust portraying Leonidas I. Royalty-free reproduction picture.

FILMS

- *The 300 Spartans.* (1962) [Film]. Rudolph Maté. Dir. USA: 20th Century Fox.
- *300.* (2006) [Film]. Zack Snyder. Dir. USA: Warner Bros.

COMMEMORATIVE BUILDINGS

- Monument to the Battle of Thermopylae, at the site of the battle (Greece).